Original title:
Can't Feel My Face, But Okay

Copyright © 2024 Creative Arts Management OÜ
All rights reserved.

Author: Elias Marchant
ISBN HARDBACK: 978-9916-94-134-8
ISBN PAPERBACK: 978-9916-94-135-5

Masked Reflections

Behind this smile, a jest hides,
I'm laughing loud, though something bides.
Got a mask on, not just for fame,
But who's to know? It's all a game.

Bubbles in my head, floating free,
Sipping on joy, who's counting me?
Face of stone, heart made of cheese,
Tickled by life, I bend with ease.

Echoes of a Numb Soul

Walking through life, a jolly stroll,
Footloose and fancy, I play my role.
Numbness wrapped in a colorful coat,
Laughing at bumps, feeling like a goat.

Echoes bounce off walls of glee,
Am I a ghost? Or just carefree?
Empty tunes in a silly dance,
Life's joke hits, in a funny trance.

Veil of Indifference

Under this veil, a grin appears,
A dichotomy wrapped in my fears.
Swallowed by mirth, I trip and fall,
Riddles of laughter, they serve me all.

Indifference wears a bright disguise,
Filled with giggles, not a single sigh.
Dancing shadows in silly hats,
What matters more, than playful chats?

The Weight of a Heart Unseen

My heart floats on, light as a feather,
Wearing a mask that says, "We're together!"
Giggles burst from a hushed embrace,
What's joy if not a silly chase?

With laughter's weight, I bounce around,
In a cloud of giggles, where fun is found.
Life's a riddle wrapped in bliss,
Can't hit the target, but who needs this?

Ghosts of Past Feelings

In the attic lies my heart,
Floating memories depart.
Laughter echoes in the gloom,
Whispers dance, they start to bloom.

Old flames flicker, lights so bright,
Turning sorrow into spite.
I trip on love's old shoelace,
Yet I smile, it's just a face.

The Art of Detachment

I juggle thoughts like playful clowns,
Pretend I wear a heavy crown.
Emotions waltz, a silly dance,
As I giggle at my own romance.

With every tear, I pour some glue,
Holding chaos like a zoo.
Letting go, a drumbeat's sway,
Pretend like it's all child's play.

Insomnia of the Spirit

Midnight snacks of feeling low,
Digesting dreams, just let them go.
Tossing, turning, wild and free,
Binge on thoughts ironically.

A pillow fight with my own head,
Whispers scream that I should tread.
Rest is fleeting, laughable plight,
Winks of madness in the night.

Chasing Shadows of Authenticity

I run with shadows, feel the chase,
Painted smiles fill the empty space.
Truth wears a mask, a game we play,
In daylight's glow, it fades away.

Hiding behind a curtain's seam,
Waves of nonsense feed the dream.
Sipping lies from a giant cup,
Finding joy as I trip up.

A Heart's Silent Surrender

My heart beats loud in silent halls,
Where laughter dances, and no one calls.
A smile slips through a velvet night,
While shadows whisper, 'It'll be alright.'

In pockets deep, I hide my tune,
Like a balloon that floats too soon.
The world spins past, I'm lost in guise,
Yet find a spark in playful eyes.

Laughing in a Language Unspoken

Bubbles rise in fizzy cheer,
With every giggle, nothing's clear.
Words tangle like spaghetti threads,
Yet joy erupts from smiling heads.

In quirky hats, we strut our stuff,
With silly puns, we've had enough!
The humor lives in every glance,
In this strange yet happy dance.

Reflections in a Distant Gaze

Mirrors giggle while I pretend,
To join this laughter without end.
Each glance a riddle, each blink a jest,
Amidst the maze, I feel so blessed.

Lost in a fog that tickles the brain,
Words escape like a runaway train.
But in the haze, I still find grace,
In the twinkle of a familiar face.

Pulse of the Unperceived

In a world where senses fade,
I dance along the masquerade.
With every pulse, a secret shared,
A fun-filled laugh where hearts are bared.

Under a ceiling of starry lights,
We weave our stories through wild nights.
Tickles linger, and smiles expand,
Lost in the beat of an unseen band.

Behind the Veil of Indifference

A grin so wide, yet chills my bones,
The laughter echoes, yet feels alone.
I dance like flames, but cold as ice,
A puppet swaying, oh, isn't that nice?

My pulse beats loud, my mask is bright,
I juggle joy, while hiding fright.
The world spins fast, I throw confetti,
But inside me, there's no confetti ready.

Witty comebacks hide the fright,
I trip on words, yet feel so light.
Behind the veil, I joke and tease,
Don't mind the frost; it's just a breeze.

Shadows of a Faded Heart

With every giggle, I fade away,

Hiding behind this jocular sway.

My heart does dances, though it's a mess,

Swirling shadows in a tight red dress.

A jester's cap, I wear with flair,

But underneath, there's just thin air.

I'm king on stage, the crowd still roars,

Yet when the lights dim, who explores?

Gravy train of laughs, I ride so fast,

Yet every joke's a spell I've cast.

In visible ink, I sign my fate,

Shadows linger, but laughter's great!

Unseen Layers of the Soul

I wear a mask, the glitter's bright,
Yet inside lurks a ghostly fright.
Underneath layers, stories untold,
Like a layered cake, but cold and old.

I toss my head and cackle loud,
To hide the silence of the crowd.
Like an onion's skin, I peel and cry,
Hoping laughter won't pass me by.

In funny hats, I twist and shout,
Yet echoes whisper what I doubt.
So spin that tale, and watch me play,
For unseen layers keep blues at bay.

The Silent Facade

In a circus of smiles, I juggle flair,
Yet in the stillness, an empty stare.
Watch me bounce, I flip and slide,
A silent facade, I wear with pride.

The world's a stage, I'm just a clown,
With floppy feet, I bounce around.
But peel the ruffles, what do you see?
A quiet face that wishes to be free.

I crack a joke, it lands with grace,
Yet shadows dance, take up my space.
Behind each laugh, I try to cope,
This silent facade, my little rope.

Limbs Lost in Limbo

My left foot dances without me,
A right arm waves hello,
Yet I'm stuck in this chair,
Am I friend or foe?

The world spins wildly around,
I laugh in delight,
With limbs that just won't budge,
What a peculiar sight!

People drift past like ghosts,
Chasing their own speed,
I'm here in frozen glory,
Watching, laugh, and feed.

Oh, how I want to join the thrill,
Yet I'm glued to this space,
My quirks are a merry show,
In this topsy-turvy race.

A Heart in Stasis

My heart is having a nap,
As life throws a party,
It's missing the grand reveal,
And yet, it feels hearty.

I smile when I shouldn't,
As joy waltzes past,
With a rhythm so lively,
My heart holds steadfast.

A beat on vacation,
While I laugh on my own,
I sing without feeling,
A king on this throne.

When the world spins in color,
And I'm stuck in a blur,
With glee, I sip my soda,
In this silent whir.

Reflections on the Edge of Emotion

I peer through the foggy glass,
Where emotions seem dense,
A smile painted on my lips,
What's all this pretense?

Joy and sorrow tango,
But I'm just a bystander,
Watching them do their flips,
While I'm a slow candor.

A laugh breaks the surface,
But beneath, I'm a stone,
Ripples of giggles abound,
Yet I'm feeling alone.

In a world of fireworks,
I'm the spark that won't flare,
Just a shiny reflection,
In the sweet summer air.

Windows to an Emotional Void

Through transparent panels,
I peer at the show,
Where laughter erupts,
And my feelings run slow.

Faces flicker like screens,
While I'm a blank slate,
A spectator of feelings,
With an odd twist of fate.

The mirth in the room,
Is a pie in the sky,
I watch it all shimmer,
With a whimsical sigh.

Yet as I float in silence,
I find solace in jest,
For the world spins on whims,
While I take a sweet rest.

Velvet Mask of Apathy

With a grin that's quite a sight,
I stroll through the day, feeling light.
Wearing comfort like a cloak,
Wrapped up tight, oh it's no joke.

Laughter echoes, but I stand still,
Shuffling thoughts with zero thrill.
A smile stuck like honey glue,
Flavors bland as morning dew.

Poking fun, I jest and play,
Yet I drift in dreamlike sway.
The world spins, a merry-go-round,
But I'm the king without a crown.

In this dance of silly glee,
I float through life, carefree,
A masked clown in afternoon light,
Where nothing shines, but all feels right.

The Taste of Nothingness

Sugar-coated dreams we chase,
Yet find only empty space.
A buffet of flavorless cheer,
Eating clouds, but nothing here.

Tickling tongues with ghostly snacks,
Our appetite gets no whacks.
A banquet void of every treat,
Where diet drinks can't even meet.

Gags of flavor-free delight,
Laughter bursts, oh what a sight!
I sip on nonsense, taste the air,
With every sip, I'm almost there.

Jokes seasoned with saltless rhyme,
In this feast, we waste our time.
But smile wide, for joy shall reign,
In this game of sweet disdain.

Driftwood Thoughts

Wandering thoughts like leaves on streams,
Catch a current, lost in dreams.
I float along with silly glee,
Like driftwood dancing endlessly.

Ideas wash up, easy to find,
Yet mixed and tangled, never aligned.
A mess of laughs in feathery hues,
Wading through this thought-filled blues.

Hang on tight to the whirling tide,
As giggles tumble, let them slide.
The winds of whimsy blow me far,
With every step, I am a star.

Bouncing thoughts like popcorn flies,
Catch me laughing under vast skies.
A treasure hunt for giggles cached,
In this world where nonsense's splashed.

In the Realm of Disconnection

In a zone where signals fade,
Chasing shadows of this charade.
I wave hello, but snooze in place,
In a world unseen, I find my grace.

Tickled by silence, laughter reigns,
As I frolic through my own chains.
Disconnected from the rush of days,
I twirl and bend through endless ways.

Whispers echo and meet thin air,
A comedy show without a care.
Fumbling beats of blushing fun,
In a realm where I'm the only one.

Giggling under a starry scheme,
In the silence, I live my dream.
Here in the void, I'm never alone,
For in this lightness, I have grown.

Whispers Beneath the Surface

I dance like a noodle, all floppy and loose,
My friends laugh and say, 'What's your excuse?'
With a grin like a globe, I tumble and sway,
But the music's all gone, in a comical way.

In this sea of lost senses, I spin and I twirl,
Like a hedgehog in high heels, watch me unfurl.
The party's alive, but I'm stuck in a phase,
With invisible giggles that sparkle and glaze.

A Canvas of Quiet

My limbs move like jelly, wobbly fun,
Painting laughter on canvases, just me and the sun.
With each jolly step, I dodge all the frowns,
Creating a masterpiece while tumbling down.

The air's full of whispers, colors abound,
But I'm lost in a bubble, no sense to be found.
As friends roll their eyes, I strike a bold pose,
I'm a work of art in a world full of prose.

The Weight of Invisible Chains

I'm weighted by giggles, encased in delight,
With every odd shimmy, I take flight.
My legs turn to spaghetti, my heart to a kite,
Floating through chuckles that brighten the night.

I trip on my thoughts, bounce off the floor,
With every misstep, they laugh even more.
I'm dragging my shadows, a cart full of glee,
Tangled in laughter, just wild and free.

Fragments of a Distant Self

I wave to the crowd, but where did I go?
A slice of confusion wrapped up in a show.
With a flick of my wrist and a bounce off the wall,
I'm the king of the circus, or maybe just small.

In this silly charade, I'm lost but I shine,
With glimmers of chaos, I'm genuinely fine.
The echoes of laughter, the sparkles I trace,
Create chunks of joy that fill up the space.

The Beauty of a Masked Heart

Behind this bright disguise, I laugh and play,
My smile's a secret, in a cheerful way.
With every silly joke, I twirl and spin,
In a bubble of joy, I'm wrapped within.

The world can't see through this painted cheer,
But giggles escape when fun friends are near.
Like a jester's cap, it bounces light,
Hiding the chaos, making it bright.

A wink, a nudge, in a game we find,
Who cares if my heart feels a little blind?
With colors and laughter, I dash through the day,
This mask is my armor, come laugh and play!

Lost in Tuneless Dances

Step to the left, then spin around,
Who needs a beat when we've got sound?
Flailing my arms like I've lost my way,
Tripping on rhythms that lead me astray.

The crowd's clapping hands, but it's all in my head,
Waltzing with shadows that dance on my bed.
My feet make a mess, but I'm grinning wide,
In this comedy show, come take a ride!

Lost in the shuffle, I stumble and sway,
With hopes that tomorrow brings better ballet.
But til then, my jig is a glorious sight,
With laughter as music, everything feels right.

Moments Lost in Translation

Words tumble awkwardly, they twist and bend,
A smile, a shrug, I'll pretend to comprehend.
In conversations, I'm sailing adrift,
The punchline's a mystery, but oh, what a gift!

Lost in a sea of mismatched phrases,
I nod and I chuckle at blank, happy gazes.
The meaning is tangled, but joy is clear,
Laughter's the language that binds us here.

We dance in the gaps, on this silly ride,
With gestures and giggles, we won't need to hide.
For in this confusion, a bond we create,
Unraveled in humor, we celebrate fate.

The Stillness of Unheard Echoes

In spaces so quiet, the shadows play games,
Whispers of chuckles, but who feels their flames?
The echoes of laughter, they bounce off the walls,
In this comedic silence, the punchline enthralls.

A nod of approval, a wink from afar,
No need for a sound, we know who we are.
In the stillness, we dance, with spirits so light,
Sharing the smiles that make dark moments bright.

Though sounds may be muted, the joy's ever bold,
In whispers of laughter, the stories unfold.
Together we revel, in silence so grand,
Finding the humor in the quietest land.

Stripped of Sensation

Nibbles of joy float by,
My cheeks are numb, oh my!
Laughter bubbles, tongue on freeze,
Gummed up giggles ride the breeze.

Why's my smile in a daze?
Tickles gone, in playful haze.
Wiggle my ears, yet can't quite hear,
Finding funny without a fear.

Pokes and prods just won't connect,
Funny faces I can't detect.
Yet here I stand, with laughter bright,
In this haze, I feel delight.

Fuzzy brain and happy flops,
Comedic turns and silly hops.
In a whirl of jolly jest,
When you're numb, just laugh the best.

Embrace of the Unfelt

Hugs that tingle like a dream,
But my arms are lost in gleam.
Wrapped in warmth without a care,
Floating freely, light as air.

Laughter echoes, though I'm numb,
Jokes fly by and still, I hum.
Each tickle brings a gentle shove,
Isn't it weird? But, oh, it's love!

Dance with shadows, sways so bright,
Invisible tunes that feel so right.
Giddy steps without the weight,
Unfeeling joy? I'll celebrate!

With a twist and silly grin,
Life's a game I wish to win.
In this swirl of undefined,
Freestyle laughter, unconfined.

Breathe Through the Void

Air tickles softly, where's the sting?
Floating here, just doing my thing.
My body's quiet, mind's a parade,
In this void, I'm unafraid.

Giggles dance in empty space,
With no sparks, but still, I chase.
Winds of humor, tease my soul,
Hollow joys that make me whole.

Join me in this enchanted game,
No touch but still, I feel the flame.
Funny vibes, a laughing miss,
Can I feel it? Oh, who needs bliss?

Twists and spins in cosmic glee,
Breathing in this reverie.
Voids can hold such jolly tunes,
I'll be the king of comic runes.

Emotions Encapsulated

My heart's a ball with no real beat,
Yet joy dances beneath my feet.
Wrapped in giggles, snug as can be,
Floating through this nonsensical spree.

Hiccups of joy, I can't forget,
Quirky feelings, a tangled net.
Unraveled jokes, silly and spry,
How did I lose my senses? Oh, my!

Twitching fingers with a grin,
Silly tales that spin and spin.
In this capsule of humor bound,
Bursts of laughter, the sweetest sound.

So bring on the puns, let them fly,
In this laughter, I will rely.
Who needs to feel when giggles bloom?
In this state, I make my room.

Melodies from a Distant Heart

When the beat drops, I'm all a-flutter,
My limbs dance like they're made of butter.
Twirling around with absent grace,
An empty smile upon my face.

A jig in boots that squeak and creak,
I laugh aloud, but can't quite speak.
My spirit's soaring, yet I'm a bit lost,
Feeling the rhythm, no matter the cost.

Jokes on me, I trip and fall,
I stumble forward, then back to the wall.
The world may turn, but here I sway,
In this comical, dizzy ballet.

Tune me up, I'll dance with flair,
My thoughts wander, are you still there?
With every wobble, I swear it's grand,
This offbeat tale, a one-man band.

A Mirror in the Fog

I checked my hair, or so I thought,
But all I saw was a what-not.
Reflections twist in a steamy haze,
No selfie here to capture the phase.

My face a puzzle, pieces astray,
A marshmallow fluff in a bright ballet.
Giggling at my own blurry game,
A hazy version of my own name.

The crusted mirror hides all my charms,
Yet I parade, like I've got no qualms.
Oh, when the haze clears, what a sight!
A face full of whimsy, laugh out loud delight.

So here I stand in my foggy show,
A lovely mess, just to let you know.
In laughter's echo, I find my way,
Through this whimsical fog, I'll dance and sway.

Fragments of What Once Was

In the corner, whispers gather dust,
Once lively tales now turn to rust.
A jigsaw puzzle without the frame,
Laughter lingers, but who's to blame?

I recall the days of dance and cheer,
When life was silly and oh-so-clear.
Now I'm left with bits and echoes,
Chasing shadows in the afterglow.

Friends with quirks, they're scattered now,
A sitcom scene with no one to bow.
The punchlines fly like paper planes,
Through the corridors of async chains.

So here I sit, a quirky recluse,
With my funny bones still on the loose.
In each fragment, a memory shines,
Navigating through these humorous lines.

The Color of Isolation

What's that hue? A dash of gray?
I wear it proudly, come what may.
A splash of laughter, a wink or grin,
An artist's canvas where I begin.

Colors blend in this solo space,
With each brush stroke, I find my pace.
Laughter bounces in empty halls,
A symphony for one, oh how it calls.

Isolation's charm is quite the plan,
Turning monotony into a dance, my friend.
With every twirl in my splattered shoes,
I paint the silence with vibrant hues.

So here I stand, my palette bright,
A burst of colors in the dead of night.
In solitude, there's still a show,
A solo act, where I steal the glow.

Driftwood on an Emotional Sea

Floating on this sea of thoughts,
My mind's a boat with wobbly knots.
Waves of joy, then splatters of gloom,
Dancing on driftwood, I can't find room.

Laughter erupts as I splash around,
While lost emotions come tumbling down.
Caught in a whirlpool of silly dreams,
Life's a punchline, bursting at the seams.

I wave at clouds in a goofy parade,
While reality's jokes are steadily played.
The tide may toss me without reprieve,
Yet on this float, I still believe.

Salty giggles under a sky of teal,
I'm adrift but hey, that's the deal!
The compass spins; where's my head?
Just wave back 'til laughter's fed!

Detachment in a Chaotic World

In a world that spins like a carnival ride,
I stroll along with my arms open wide.
Giddy chaos finds me in the fray,
Yet I float through like it's a fun day.

People rush by, lost in their race,
While I munch popcorn, enjoying the space.
Confetti storms in each wild direction,
I chuckle, yes, this is pure perfection.

The jester within shares quirky wisdom,
"Detach a bit, join in the rhythm!"
With each belly laugh, I trip and sway,
Laughter's the glue in this strange ballet.

In this circus, where tears might flow,
I balance on tightropes that nobody knows.
With an exaggerated wink, I proclaim,
Detachment's a game, and I'm winning the fame!

Unraveled Yet Unbroken

Threads of chaos dangle from my seams,
While I juggle life's outrageous dreams.
In this fabric of fancy, I twist and twine,
Snagged by stitches, but oh, I feel fine!

My socks don't match, but who even cares?
I skip through the mess like it's full of airs.
Life's a patchwork of colors gone wild,
With a melody sweet as a mischief-loving child.

Unraveled and tangled, a vivid delight,
I dance in the chaos, wearing it right.
Each little snag is a story to tell,
In this topsy-turvy world, I fit well.

Even when threads start to fray and split,
I laugh at the irony; isn't it a hit?
In this quilt of life, I'm joyful, unbroken,
With every free stitch a tale left unspoken.

The Phantom Embrace

In the shadows, a tickle and tease,
A phantom's hug, oh so hard to seize.
I'm wrapped up tight yet floating away,
Ignoring the quirks of this wild ballet.

Ghostly giggles echo in my mind,
As I trip over laughter, so hard to find.
With invisible arms that give me a whirl,
Every moment's a tumble in a fun, odd swirl.

In this wacky waltz, the world disappears,
Absurdities dance with my silly fears.
Embraced by a jest that just won't let go,
I twirl through the mist with a comical glow.

Phantom hugs come with a crazy flair,
A chuckle and tumble fill the air.
So I sway with laughter, if only in jest,
In this odd embrace, I'm thoroughly blessed!

A Dream Between Awareness

In a world where colors play,
I'd wear mismatched socks all day.
Ice cream melts in swirling skies,
Laughing while my donut cries.

Imagined friends in vibrant hats,
Juggling dreams with playful bats.
Ticklish thoughts, a sudden sneeze,
Giggles escape like dancing bees.

Lively tunes from nowhere burst,
Quirky shapes that quench my thirst.
As shadows dance, I spin around,
Caught in joy, I lose all ground.

Tick-tock clocks, they twirl and flip,
Time's a ride, I take a dip.
Floating on a cloud of cheese,
Life's a puzzle, strange but ease.

Shadows of a Heartbeat

A heartbeat echoes, soft and sweet,
As shadows waltz on tiny feet.
With silly hats and blushing cheeks,
I speak in rhymes, like playful freaks.

Nonsense tales of frogs in ties,
Winking stars that giggle and sigh.
Chasing clouds, we race the breeze,
Wearing socks smeared with cheese.

My heart does backflips on the street,
While squirrels challenge me to beat.
Dancing shadows, oh what a sight,
Underneath the moon's soft light.

Whispers float and butterflies tease,
In this land where laughter sees.
I wave goodbye to worries near,
With every chuckle, joy draws near.

Walking Through Foggy Memory

In foggy realms where memories play,
I trip on thoughts that slip away.
A dapper cat with googly eyes,
Navigates through marshmallow skies.

Forgotten notes in jars of jam,
Remind me of a quiet clam.
With every step, a giggle goes,
Like silly socks on dancing toes.

Slipping on banana peels,
As laughter spins like clumsy wheels.
Floating past on rainbow trails,
This foggy dream is where joy sails.

Through twisting paths I trot then leap,
In this haze, my heart takes a sweep.
Embracing whispers on the run,
Chasing giggles, oh what fun!

The Taste of Lingering Absence

A taste of cotton candy air,
Sweeter than my mom's old chair.
It vanishes like silly smoke,
Leaving traces of a joke.

With every bite, I float and twirl,
Tickled pink, in a whirl.
Absence flavors every jest,
Hidden well, I'm on a quest.

Like sprinkles on a birthday cake,
I laugh at every small mistake.
In this flavor of the night,
Silly dreams take playful flight.

Yet in the shadows, laughter rings,
As joy unfurls on paper wings.
Wrapped in smiles, I take a chance,
To twirl and dance in my own trance.

Shadows Without Substance

In the mirror, just a grin,
A ghostly grin, where do I begin?
The laughter echoes, but I don't feel,
Like a cartoon, it's all surreal.

Jokes fly by like paper planes,
My body's here, but where's the brain?
Dancing with shadows in my head,
A party's on, but I'm not fed.

Punchlines land but bounce away,
A game of charades, come what may.
My limbs move with a wobbly sway,
Who needs senses? Let's laugh and play!

Waves of giggles, I ride the tide,
But deep inside, I can't confide.
A silly show, I wave goodbye,
A mask I wear, just to comply.

Tracing Emotions in Silence

Silent whispers fill the air,
A tangled web of joy and despair.
I mime a laugh, I stretch a smile,
But deep inside, it's been a while.

Fingers dance, but chords don't play,
A soundtrack lost along the way.
The awkward moments seem to shine,
Like misplaced socks in a laundry line.

I juggle thoughts, a clownish act,
With heartbeats that feel almost packed.
But every chuckle's just a ruse,
Note to self: what did I lose?

In this circus, I take my bow,
With fabric that doesn't quite allow.
A funny face in a blank expanse,
Yet somehow still, I join the dance.

The Art of Disconnection

Wi-Fi lost, but jokes are found,
Disconnected from the merry sound.
I laugh too loud, it echoes back,
An empty room with giggles on track.

Messages sent but no replies,
A ghosting party in disguise.
I break the silence with a cheer,
But my own voice just disappears.

In the gallery of idle time,
I paint with words, but miss the rhyme.
Sipping laughter in a coffee cup,
I'm wide awake, but feeling stuck.

The art I make is bittersweet,
Like shoes that pinch yet feel so neat.
I'll take a bow with a shaky stance,
In this odd world, I'll take a chance.

Behind the Curtain of Apathy

Behind the veil, a jester's grin,
Where apathy's tune begins to spin.
I crack a joke, but where's the jest?
Sitting with clouds on my fuzzy vest.

My mind's a stage, but the play's a flop,
A humor fest, but I'll never stop.
Punchlines missed in a spun-out loop,
In a world that feels like chicken soup.

I juggle dreams that float away,
While laughter hums a muted sway.
A curtain's wave, and then I blink,
What was that thought? I need a drink!

With giggles hiding behind my chest,
I wear my mask; is this the best?
A show of smiles with empty grace,
Behind it all, a missing face.

Painted Smiles

With colors bright, we wear the grin,
A mask so sweet, where do we begin?
Our laughter echoes, a joyful cheer,
While inside whispers, 'Is anyone near?'

With gloss and glitter, we dance around,
In circles so wide, our troubles abound.
A wink and a nod, we play our part,
Chasing the sun, hiding the heart.

Hollow Hearts

In a room full of chatter, silence speaks,
Like bubbles of joy that pop with shrieks.
We toast with smiles, while bodies sway,
Yet inside we ponder, just passing the day.

Our jokes fly high, like kites on a string,
Yet tethered below, it doesn't feel spring.
With every chuckle, a tear we hide,
Behind laughter's armor, the shadows slide.

The Weight of Unseen Burdens

Like backpacks loaded with bricks and stones,
We laugh so loud, but hear muffled moans.
A belly full of giggles, a heart weighed down,
In the land of the jester, we wear the crown.

Our burdens wobble, we sway and dance,
Yet underneath smiles, we barely prance.
When the lights go dim, we drop the play,
Cocooned in shadows, we drift away.

Laughter Behind Closed Doors

Behind the curtains, the fun resumes,
Where echoes of joy replace the glooms.
With pratfalls and puns, we let it all out,
As neighbors wonder what it's all about.

In a sanctuary built of giggles and lore,
We dance like fools on the living room floor.
Yet outside the world spins with frowns and sighs,
While we conjure magic with laughter and lies.

Colors Lacking Vigor

We paint the walls with shades of delight,
But brush strokes fade when fades the light.
Our canvas bright, yet feels so gray,
As laughter slips through, just slips away.

We splash around in hues so wide,
Yet miss the spark that once was inside.
In this gallery of funny grace,
We find the bliss, yet lose the base.

Lost Connections

Lost in a crowd, yet alone,
Time ticks by like a stone.
Smiles float by on a breeze,
But I'm stuck in my unease.

A nod here and a wink there,
My head spins, I'm unaware.
Hands wave as if to say,
Is this a party or a play?

Voices drown out the beat,
Like whispers of deceit.
I laugh as I trip on air,
These moments lead to nowhere.

In the chaos, I must jest,
A jester in a funny fest.
With every twist and turn,
I find the joy I yearn.

Energy Adrift

Floating like a balloon,
Swaying to an unknown tune.
Bouncing off the walls and floor,
Yet craving something more.

Giggles echo, shadows dance,
Lost in this hilarious trance.
Wobbling as I take a sip,
Grinning wide, I'm on a trip.

Waves of giggles crash on me,
Like a storm upon the sea.
I'm carried in a frothy wave,
To places wild and brave.

Each laugh holds a reckless grace,
In this unpredictable space.
With every slip and slide,
I embrace the joyful ride.

Heartbeats in Stillness

A tick-tock fills the air,
Moments dance without a care.
I search for rhythm, can't catch a sigh,
My heart skips, oh, my, oh my!

A beat that feels like a joke,
As I stumble, gasp, and choke.
Smiling through the silent spree,
What's wrong with my melody?

In a room full of glee,
I grin like it's all meant to be.
Swaying like a banner flown,
Though the music's not my own.

Yet I laugh, "This beats all!"
With each echo, I stand tall.
Really, who needs the trace,
When laughter has its own place?

The Chill of an Empty Pulse

A chill creeps under my skin,
As friends laugh, let the fun begin.
Like a cartoon dropped in lime,
I bounce through this quirky rhyme.

The air is thick, yet I'm so light,
Numbness spins; it's quite a sight.
I trip and tumble, yet I grin,
In this silliness, I win.

A blank slate in a vibrant scene,
Floating like I'm in a dream.
Life's a game of peek-a-boo,
I play along, yes, it's true.

With each chuckle, I grow bold,
In this frosty tale retold.
Who needs a pulse when a laugh will do,
In this funny world, I'm brand new!

When Touch Becomes a Dream

I reached out to grab a fluff,
Only to clutch an empty puff.
The world around me feels so light,
Like I'm dancing with ghosts tonight.

My friends all laugh, they call my name,
I nod along, but it's a game.
I wave my hands in silly spins,
Pretending I'm back where it begins.

A high five missed, a hug that's not,
A bouncy castle of a thought.
A tickle fight turns into air,
With every glance, I feel the flare.

So here I am, a silken breeze,
Gliding through moments with such ease.
In this odd dance of bold charade,
I'm the jester, unafraid.

Whispers of a Fading Presence

A echo bounces through the room,
A crooked grin hides all my gloom.
I try to speak but lose my tongue,
The laughter calls, the song's unsung.

With every joke, I trip and fall,
I'm just a shadow on the wall.
A wisp of hair, a flicker bright,
A phantom mixed with pure delight.

They say I'm here, but who's to know?
A wacky dance, a silly show.
The music plays, but I'm not there,
Just floating whispers in the air.

So join me in this hazy cheer,
And let's pretend we've conquered fear.
In this strange game of hide-and-seek,
I'm invisible, but laughter's peak.

The Silence Hides the Storm

The quiet hums, it sings along,
With every silence, I feel strong.
A wink and nod, my heart's aglow,
In quiet spots, I steal the show.

The world outside begins to swirl,
A merry dance, a twirl and whirl.
I twiddle thumbs, play with my hair,
A masterpiece of empty air.

Among the chatter, I make my stand,
I'd join the troupe, if I had a hand.
Yet here I flop, in dreams I leap,
Through giggles shared, the secrets keep.

This hush misleads the eye so sly,
Yet laughter leaps as moments fly.
Round and round we skip the norm,
Caught in the swirl, a soft, warm storm.

Invisible Threads of Existence

I wove a tale of fun and jest,
With invisible seams, I feel blessed.
A string of joy, forever tight,
Pulling me close in endless flight.

A nudge from nowhere makes me grin,
The clocks all stop, let games begin.
A staged performance on this stage,
In every pause, I feel the rage.

The world spins wild, a dizzy ride,
As I float on dreams, I cannot hide.
A friend of air, a buddy of light,
We crack up at our silly plight.

So here I roll, in laughs we weave,
In this wild dance, I do believe.
The threads of laughter hold us fast,
In this moment's joy, we're unsurpassed.

Fable of the Forgotten Touch

In a world of tickles and forgotten charms,
Where laughter dances without any alarms,
I lost the sense of a playful tickle,
Now I just chuckle at each silly pickle.

My cheeks are grinning, but can't quite feel,
Like riding a rollercoaster with no wheel,
Jokes fly by, I mimic their flair,
Like a clown with a nose but an empty stare.

Hands up in the air, yet nothing is felt,
Just a jolly jig with a spicy sundelt,
Waves of giggles wash over the plain,
While my senses misbehave like a runaway train.

So here I stand, a puppet all geared,
Laughing at moments that the heart once steered,
Oh, fable quite funny, with quirks I parade,
In the land of the unfeeling, I'm still quite displayed.

Captive of the Unfelt

A jester in chains of invisible strings,
Where whispers of laughter are all that it brings,
My heart skips beats, but no thrum around,
A statue of joy that's forever unwound.

I order a hug, yet no one arrives,
With a smile that glows, but my soul barely thrives,
Like ketchup on chips that never will blend,
The punchlines are heard, yet no twinkle to send.

I trip and I fall, but it's just for the scene,
Falling in laughter, my fingers still clean,
Behold the absurdity, no feel to embarrass,
Just a goofy grin, in this life sans the lavish.

So cheers to the moments, both wacky and wild,
For I'm still quite the joker, albeit a mild,
In the captive of unfeeling, I'll make my own cheer,
With no touch to recall, yet a heart full of beer.

In the Realm of Emotion's Ghost

In a haunted hall where feelings retreat,
I'm dancing with shadows, a humorous feat,
The poltergeist giggles, but I'm not alone,
We share in the jest of a lived-over zone.

Ticklish whispers flit past my ear,
While I pose as a statue, void of all fear,
The ghost of a grin haunts the air in between,
Making fun of the fun that's never been seen.

Like bubbles that pop without any sound,
I prance through the atmosphere, floaty and round,
Where laughter is written on pages of fluff,
The paper's unscripted, but I'm getting tough.

So here in this realm, I twirl and I sway,
With jesters and wraiths, we frolic and play,
In the land of the ghost where emotions run free,
I'll laugh with the breezes, it's just you and me.

The Journey Without Feelings

On a train of giggles, I rise with great cheer,
Chugging along tracks that aren't ever clear,
With every whoosh, the air is a tease,
I may not feel, but I'm still the breeze.

Passengers chuckle, though I sit bland,
Playing the role of a rubber-band stand,
Each punchline delivered, a whoopee disguise,
In a world of emotions that quietly flies.

I wave at the clouds with a whimsical grin,
For each drop of joy feels like water in sin,
A journey so merry, though none are at play,
I'll ride this train through the jest of the day.

At the end of my travel, I'll burst into shine,
With a laugh that's crafted from nonsense divine,
For the fun is alive in this space I adore,
On a journey with jest, who could ask for more?

Lingering Between Two Worlds

I'm all dressed up, but where's the flair?
My mind's on a trip, while I'm stuck in a chair.
The mirror's reflection gives me a wink,
Am I here for the party or lost in a drink?

Jokes from the crowd buzz like a bee,
But I'm floating so high, just as carefree.
A laugh escapes, then it fizzles out,
Like a balloon that forgot how to shout.

My heart's a DJ, spinning the tunes,
Yet my feet feel heavy, like concrete balloons.
I bob my head, but where'd my groove go?
Oh look, there it is, in the chips on the low.

I'm in a dance-off, but forgot the step,
Making it up, I begin to prep.
Between the worlds, I twirl and bend,
Is this just me, or did I lose a trend?

Wraiths of Emotion

Here comes a feeling, like a ghost on parade,
Floating around, my smile mismade.
A tickle of laughter, a sprinkle of tears,
Oh wait, was that someone? Or just my weird fears?

I wear my joy like a funny disguise,
With silly jokes and glassy-eyed sighs.
The world spins on, and I cling to the ride,
While chaos waltzes in, comically wide.

Who knew that thoughts could feel like a dance?
A shimmy, a shake, just missing romance.
While giggles become my best-kept chant,
Reality checks out; I'm off to the slant.

So here's to the mood swings, wraiths of delight,
That tickle my ribs while I'm feeling light.
In shadows of laughter, I stand and I sway,
What's reality? It's more fun this way!

Melodies of the Unheard

In a room full of chatter, I'm stuck in my tune,
The beat of my heart's like a wild cartoon.
Everyone's dancing, but I'm in a hum,
Life's a symphony, but I'm playing a drum.

Lyrics are lost, in a whimsical fog,
I'm the lone ballad, a quirky old dog.
The notes of the night twirl and twist around,
While I'm here just giggling, on this silly ground.

With melodies swirling in colors so bright,
I'm a jester at large, under the moonlight.
The rhythm's contagious, I can't help but sway,
Though keys might be missing, I'm okay with the play.

So let's raise a toast to the tunes that we forge,
With laughter and joy, we'll never lose charge.
In a land where the unheard becomes purest delight,
We're dancing in silence, under stars shining bright.

A Diary of the Dimming

Sometimes I wonder if I'm real or a dream,
Writing a diary by the glow of the beam.
Words tumble out, like a jumbled old game,
Where fears take a seat, but the laughs are aflame.

Pages turning with a grin and a wink,
Between the lines, my thoughts start to sink.
A chuckle or two at my antics within,
As I dance with the moon while the daylight grows thin.

I write about moments, both fuzzy and clear,
Where laughter collides with the depths of my fear.
But what could be lost in a diary's light,
Ends up in giggles, shadowed by night.

So here's to the whimsy, the spill of the ink,
As I pen down the tales of my thoughts on the brink.
In this diary of dimming, every laugh is a score,
A reminder that fun is an open door.

Diary of a Distant Echo

I shout into the void and wait,
A silly sound returns, but late.
My nose is tingling, is it the air?
Or just my hair doing a wacky dare?

I trip over my own two feet,
A dance with gravity, quite the feat.
Laughter bubbles, fills the room,
As I glance down at my mismatched shoes' doom.

With whimsy in my steps today,
I juggle thoughts, but they slip away.
Echos of giggles bounce around,
In this wild circus, I'm the clown renowned.

So here's to the echoes, bright and loud,
In a comical life, I stand proud.
Reality's a jest, I'm just the guy,
With a grin so wide, I might just fly.

The Heart's Hidden Reverie

My heart beats like a funky drum,
In beats so odd, they sound quite dumb.
A rhythm that refuses straight lines,
It sways and jiggles like wobbly vines.

I chase the dreams that slip away,
Like soap bubbles on a sunny day.
They pop with giggles when I get too close,
Leaving me chasing a shimmering ghost.

With whispers of nonsense in the air,
I dance with shadows, full of flair.
Playful thoughts in a chaotic swirl,
Embracing the spin, oh what a whirl!

So here's to the laughter and silly spins,
In the dreamland where absurdity wins.
My heart's a joker, and I'm its fool,
Riding the waves of this whimsical pool.

Awash in Hazy Horizons

In foggy fields where giggles bloom,
A clumsy jogger stumbles with gloom.
Hazy horizons hide the fun,
Like a game of peek-a-boo with the sun.

I can't quite see just what's ahead,
But I'm dressed like a rainbow, enough said.
With mismatched socks and two different shoes,
Dancing away with no time to lose.

The sun's a cheerleader, bright and bold,
While I cartwheel awkwardly, uncontrolled.
At any moment, I might take flight,
Or trip on fairy dust, what a sight!

So I laugh with the clouds, drift where they sway,
In a hazy world, we'll play all day.
For fun is a treasure no map can chart,
And joy is the journey that fills the heart.

Traces of a Detached Spirit

Floating around like a wayward balloon,
I wave at the stars, they sing a tune.
My thoughts are taffy, stretching so long,
In a bubble of giggles, where I belong.

With sparkles of whimsy, I spin and glide,
Amongst the shadows, I take a ride.
I slip on boisterous dreams, quite absurd,
Whispering secrets that never were heard.

So I dance with the quirks of the night,
Tickled by starlight, feeling so light.
A playful spirit in a whimsical chase,
In the laughter of echoes, I find my place.

Now watch as I twirl with mischievous grace,
In this funny world, I've carved out my space.
Detached yet enchanted, I prance and play,
For joy is the path, come join the sway!

Fog in a Fractured Mirror

Reflections twist, a game of chance,
My smile's missing, but I still dance.
Laughter echoes, like a distant hum,
In a world that's fuzzy, but still so fun.

Waves of giggles slip through the haze,
Chasing the shadows in a playful maze.
Eyes wide open, but they seem to glaze,
Navigating life's quirky gaze.

Chuckling softly at the jest,
I wear my joy like a fluffy vest.
Through cloudy thoughts, I roam and play,
In this wobbly world, I'll find my way.

So here's to the fog, the jumbled lines,
To fractured mirrors and joyful signs.
I can't quite grasp, but I won't despair,
In this funny haze, there's magic to share.

When Touch is Just a Memory

Fingers reaching, but just thin air,
A ghostly brush, a whimsical scare.
I wave at shadows, they wave back slow,
A dance with whispers, a frolic in tow.

Once solid hugs, now float away,
Like cotton candy on a breezy day.
I laugh at warmth that's lost in the past,
In this playful drift, I'll have a blast.

The tickle of laughter, a fleeting tease,
While ticklish ghosts spin round with ease.
Memory lingers, a sweet little game,
As I reach out to touch, but find it's the same.

So here I stand, in echoing glee,
Where feel and real play hide and seek.
I might be lost, but joy's in the chase,
In a world where memory comes to embrace.

Silence Wrapped in Empty Words

Whispers flutter like butterflies pale,
Wrapped in silence, they giggle and wail.
I speak in riddles, you nod and grin,
In this realm of echoes, where do we begin?

Words float around like balloons on high,
They pop and vanish, oh me, oh my!
We laugh at the void, so light and bright,
In this silly dance, we take flight.

Empty promises, oh what a sight,
Like popcorn kernels bouncing with delight.
Each chuckle bubbles, a fizzy spree,
In this carnival of nonsensical glee.

So let's celebrate this playful void,
Where silence reigns but joy's not destroyed.
In a world of echoes, we'll find our tune,
Laughing at shadows, beneath the moon.

The Chilling Embrace of Stillness

In quiet corners, the laughter stirs,
A pause in motion, where joy occurs.
The stillness wraps like a cozy quilt,
In this frozen frame, our laughter's built.

I stand like a statue, feeling afar,
But inside I'm zipping like a shining star.
The chilly air holds secrets and glee,
As I bounce in place, wild and free.

Silent chuckles flit on the breeze,
A world of wonder, just aim to please.
In this frosty space, we twirl and sway,
Where laughter glimmers, come what may.

So let's toast to stillness, to laughs that freeze,
In the cool embrace, where joy's a tease.
Among the quiet, the fun is alive,
In the chilling calm, we're meant to thrive.

Beneath the Masks We Wear

A smile plastered, bright and wide,
Underneath, I seem to hide.
Laughter bubbles, then it spills,
Nonsense tales, oh what a thrill!

With quirks and giggles, we disguise,
In this jester's world, we rise.
Behind the laughter, oops, who knew?
We dance along, a merry crew!

We juggle jokes, we hop and prance,
With serious faces—not a chance!
As silly thoughts wander astray,
We cheer each moment, come what may!

So here's to masks, to silly games,
In joyful folly, we claim our names.
With every twist and every turn,
We find the light, and brightly burn.

Serenity in the Void

In quiet chaos, joy takes flight,
Where empty moments spark delight.
The silence sings, no words to share,
Just quirky grins and vacant stares.

Under the moon, we tread so light,
With moonlit pranks, we chase the night.
A spacious void, where laughter flows,
In empty corners, humor grows.

We waltz on air, we skip on dreams,
Through radiant beams and twilight gleams.
A cosmic joke, this vast expanse,
In solitude, we take our chance.

So here we lay, in endless jest,
Finding joy in the pointless quest.
Among the stars, we laugh and sway,
In empty bliss, we find our way.

Masked Whispers

Behind the veil, a giggle hides,
With whispers soft, the madness rides.
In secret glances, laughter flows,
Unmasked joy, that nobody knows.

Our faces say what hearts can't show,
In silly tones, we let it go.
With quirks and quirks, we spin the tale,
In every silence, jokes prevail.

Through playful nods and winks we share,
The blissful jest in the open air.
In every chuckle, a spark ignites,
Creating mirth through endless nights.

So raise your glass, let's toast the game,
With masked whispers that sound the same.
In every jest, we find our way,
Dancing lightly as we sway.

Echoes of Emotionless Nights

In stillness, echoes bounce around,
In endless loops, no need for sound.
With grins and chuckles, we play the part,
Of laughter stirring the frozen heart.

Late night murmurs, to the stars we speak,
With silly dreams that seem so bleak.
Not all is lost as humor sways,
In flickering lights, we dance and play.

Oh, time stands still, but we move fast,
Through humor's realm, we'll ever last.
With every quirk, our spirits rise,
As we navigate the comic skies.

So here's to nights, where humor reigns,
In echoes soft, we break the chains.
With smiles unmasked, we embrace the fun,
In laughter's light, we are all one.

Words Unspoken

Jokes hang like curtains, nowhere to land,
My laughter's a silence, an awkward stand.
Trying to speak, but the words slip away,
I chuckle and nod, in my own silly way.

Puns fall like feathers, lost in the air,
Each pun I can't feel, but I pretend to care.
My tongue is a candy, all covered in fluff,
Now sweet like a joke, but it feels kinda rough.

Feelings Unsensed

A tickle of humor that never arrives,
I giggle at shadows that waltz and jive.
Punchlines evade like an elusive ghost,
I'm jesting alone, is this what I boast?

Inside of my head, the banter runs free,
But outside it's static, where could it be?
I dance with the echoes, a wobbly sway,
With laughter as my guide, I'll open the way.

Ghosts of Past Desires

Old crushes like specters that haunt and tease,
The memories shimmer, drift on the breeze.
What once was a spark now feels like a chill,
Yet I twirl in the past, and I can't take my fill.

Flirting with phantoms, it's all in good fun,
Their shadows are playful, and I'm on the run.
Laughter erupts like bubbles in air,
With each wistful thought, I can't help but stare.

The Numb Beneath the Surface

Beneath all the giggles, a numbness at play,
While my heart does a jig, my mind drifts away.
A smile painted on, like a mask made of clay,
What's lost in the laughter, I choice not to say.

Ping-ponging thoughts, like a ball on the floor,
I bounce back and forth, but I'm wanting much more.
The jests keep me floating, but do I feel fine?
When the punchline drops hard, is the laughter still mine?

Emotions Entombed

Deep down in the vault where my chuckles reside,
Things simmer and bubble, but I try to hide.
With a grin in the mirrors reflecting my face,
Something stirs within, but it stays in its place.

Wrapped tight like a mummy, my feelings all sealed,
Each joke that I crack is a sliver revealed.
I laugh at the nonsense in silly disguise,
While buried beneath are the truths and the lies.

Glimmers of Forgotten Joy

In a world where laughter lurks,
Falling flat like silly quirks.
I dance with shadows, oh so bright,
Chasing giggles in the night.

Mismatched socks and hefty grins,
Twisting tales where silliness begins.
Each step a stumble, a playful race,
Who needs the map? Let's lose our place!

Invisible splashes freeze the scene,
Plastic smiles in spaces unseen.
Life tickles the funny bone, it seems,
Wrapped in delicious, dreamlike dreams.

In the chaos, joy gently weaves,
Through comic strips and autumn leaves.
Here's to moments that bring delight,
Funny feelings take flight tonight!

Buried Beneath a Surface

A rubber chicken leads the way,
Underneath the play, we sway.
Banana peels and bubble gum
Hide the giggles, here we come!

On a rollercoaster of delight,
Belly-laughs take off in flight.
From towering waves of giggling glee,
To little hiccups that set us free.

Underneath this silly shell,
Smirks and chuckles ring the bell.
Each glance exchanged, a jest untold,
Like glitter hidden in the fold.

The surface gleams, but underneath,
Laughter twirls, like fallen leaves.
Pull the strings of joy once more,
Who knew silliness could explore?

The Other Side of Touch

A tickle here, a poke right there,
Invisible bonds that fill the air.
Like whispers caught in silly pout,
Laughter's journey knows no doubt.

Slapstick falls and friendly shoves,
A dance that fits like hand-in-gloves.
With hugs made of rubbery cheer,
We find a groove that disappears.

When fingers wave and noses dance,
Silly antics spark a chance.
That warmth we crave is quite absurd,
A giggle shared, a sweetly stirred.

Behind the touch, the laughs collide,
In bumpy rides, we slip and slide.
Wrapped in joy, we'll learn to clutch,
Life's thrilling ride, the other touch!

Shadows Speak Louder

Shadows stretch and twist away,
Turning silence into play.
With every grin, the world ignites,
Silly whispers in the night.

A misstep here, a nouveau cha-cha,
Giggles ringing like a mantra.
We weave our tales, absurd and wild,
Like dreams unfurling, free and styled.

Unseen sketches paint the ground,
Mirth flows free, like laughter bound.
Through the twilight, joy's parade,
Mingle in the silliness we've made.

In the whispers, shadows peep,
Awakening secrets we all keep.
With each chuckle, we rediscover,
Life's funny dance, like no other!

Milton Keynes UK
Ingram Content Group UK Ltd.
UKHW021349011224
451618UK00023B/221